12 IMMIGRANTS WHO MADE
AMERICAN
POLITICS GREAT

by Diane Marczely Gimpel

www.12StoryLibrary.com

12-Story Library is an imprint of Bookstaves.

Photographs ©: JOYCE NALTCHAYAN/AFP/Getty Images, cover, 1; John Trumbull/PD, 4; The Bureau of Engraving and Printing/PD, 5; Jack R Perry Photography/Shutterstock.com, 5; United States Department of State, 6; Carolyn Kaster/Associated Press, 7; US House Office of Photography, 8; Tom Williams/CQ Roll Call/Associated Press, 9; Library of Congress, 10; Associated Press, 11; US Department of Transportation, 12; Office of the President-elect/ CC4.0, 13; US Department of Transportation, 13; Small Business Administration/PD, 14; GES 2016/PD, 15; US Department of State, 16; US Information Agency, 17; Renee Bouchard/US Senate Photographic Studio, 18; Alexandra Hemmerly-Brown/US Army, 19; Dale Frost of the Port of San Diego/CC2.0, 20; mark reinstein/Shutterstock.com, 21; Leopaltik1242/CC4.0, 22; Carlos Gonzalez/ZUMA Press/Newscom, 23; Loomis Dean/The LIFE Picture Collection/ Getty Images, 24; Jon R. Friedman/PD, 25; US Congress, 26; Chip Somodevilla/Getty Images, 27; Fekist/CC4.0, 27; The Bureau of Engraving and Printing/PD, 28; US National Archives and Records Administration, 29

ISBN
978-1-63235-575-1 (hardcover)
978-1-63235-629-1 (paperback)
978-1-63235-690-1 (ebook)

Library of Congress Control Number: 2018947549

Printed in the United States of America
Mankato, MN
June 2018

About the Cover
Madeleine Albright in 2000.

Access free, up-to-date content on this topic plus a full digital version of this book. Scan the QR code on page 31 or use your school's login at 12StoryLibrary.com.

Table of Contents

Alexander Hamilton Helps Found the United States

Alexander Hamilton was born in the 1750s on Nevis. This small island in the Caribbean Sea was a British colony. Hamilton's family was poor. He had to get a job early in life. As a teen, he was a store clerk. He managed the money. Hamilton was so good at his job that the store owner sent him to college New York.

Hamilton arrived in Boston, Massachusetts, in 1772. It was a tense time in the American colonies. Many people wanted to break free from British rule. In 1775, the colonies went to war with England. Hamilton wanted independence. He joined the army. Soon he became an advisor to General George Washington.

The colonists won the war in 1783. The United States became an independent country. But the government was weak. Hamilton and others believed it should be stronger. In 1787, leaders met in Philadelphia. At the meeting, the US Constitution was written. This document would create a stronger central government. But first it had to be ratified by 9 of the 13 states. Hamilton wrote essays to help. The Constitution was ratified in 1788.

George Washington became the first US president in 1789. He chose

Official portrait of Alexander Hamilton, the first US Secretary of the Treasury.

Hamilton to be the first secretary of the US Treasury. In that job, Hamilton helped manage the new country's money. It was a hard job. The United States had a lot of debt. New financial systems had to be created. But Hamilton persisted. By the time he stepped down, Hamilton had helped strengthen the US government and economy.

11
Hamilton's age, in years, when he started working.

- Hamilton's ability to manage money helped him attend college in the American colonies.
- Hamilton fought against the British during the American Revolution.
- After independence, he helped strengthen the government and economy.

Madeleine Albright Is First Female US Secretary of State

The Albright family fled to England. Because they were Jewish, they worried the invading Nazis would hurt them.

After the war, the Albrights moved back to their home country. They would not stay long, however. Communists took control of the government in 1948. The Albright family fled again, this time to the United States. Madeleine was 11 years old.

In the United States, Madeleine Albright went to high school in Denver, Colorado. There she founded an international relations club. She was very interested in how countries got along with each other. In college, Albright was active in politics and government.

Madeleine Albright understood from a young age how a country's actions affect people's lives. Her family lived in the present-day Czech Republic. But they could not stay. Germany invaded the country at the beginning of World War II in 1939.

In 1993, President Bill Clinton made Albright the US Ambassador to the United Nations. The United Nations

6
Number of years World War II lasted (1939–1945).

- The Albright family emigrated from the Czech Republic to escape Nazism and communism.
- Albright served as US Ambassador to the United Nations.
- She became the first female US Secretary of State in 1997.

is a group of people from countries around the world. It works to make the world better. Albright helped the group end world conflicts and promote peace.

Four years later, Albright was named US Secretary of State. She was now in charge of handling the United

President Obama awards Albright the Presidential Medal of Freedom in 2012.

States' relationships with other countries. Albright is the first woman to hold that job. Over the next four years, she worked to protect the nation and make the world more peaceful.

Pramila Jayapal Is First Indian American Congresswoman

University and Northwestern University.

After college, Jayapal worked in New York City. Her job was to study how well businesses managed their money. Jayapal was good at her work, but she decided to dedicate her life to helping others.

In 2001, Jayapal started an organization in Seattle, Washington, that benefited immigrants. Called OneAmerica, it helped new citizens register to vote. The organization also pushed for laws that are fair to people who immigrate to the United States.

Pramila Jayapal was born in Chennai, India, in 1965. As a teenager, she moved to the United States to attend college. Jayapal earned degrees at Georgetown

Jayapal's work has not only benefited immigrants. She was part of a group that worked to raise the minimum wage in Seattle. The minimum wage is the lowest amount of money a worker can earn for each hour worked. A higher minimum

Rep. Pramila Jayapal marching in support of immigrants, June, 2018.

wage can improve the lives of working people.

In 2013, the Obama White House named her a Champion of Change.

People in Washington State also recognized how Jayapal was helping people. In 2014, voters chose her to serve in the state senate. Two years later, Jayapal was elected to the US House of Representatives. She is the first Indian American woman to be elected to that post.

15
Amount of the minimum wage Jayapal fought for, in dollars per hour.

- Jayapal emigrated from India to attend college in the United States.
- After working in business, she began focusing on how she could help people in need.
- Jayapal became the first Indian American woman in the House of Representatives.

Felix Frankfurter Serves on US Supreme Court

When he was 22, Frankfurter went to a speech by Louis Brandeis. This famous lawyer said it was important to defend people in need. The speech by the "people's lawyer" inspired Frankfurter to want to work for the public good.

One way Frankfurter served was to help start the American Civil Liberties Union. Since 1920, this organization has used court cases to protect personal freedoms.

Felix Frankfurter grew up with injustice all around him. His family was Jewish. In Vienna, Austria, that meant being mistreated. Many people there were prejudiced against Jewish people in the late 1800s.

In 1894, the Frankfurter family moved to New York City. Felix was 12 at the time. In the United States, he attended a public city school. After graduating, Frankfurter decided to study law.

Soon after law school, Frankfurter got a job in a federal court. In this role, he helped US presidents make important decisions. He also worked to preserve people's rights. In 1939, President Franklin D. Roosevelt named Frankfurter to the US Supreme Court. On this highest court, Frankfurter helped decided whether US laws were constitutional.

Frankfurter also helped to integrate schools. At the time, some Southern states forced black children and

LITTLE ROCK CENTRAL HIGH

RAY

ROBERTS

PATTILLO

THOMAS

WALLS

MOTHERSHED

BROWN

ECKFORD

GREEN

The nine students who were escorted into school by the National Guard after the Supreme Court's 1954 decision.

23
Number of years Felix Frankfurter served on the US Supreme Court.

- Frankfurter's family emigrated from Austria to escape mistreatment.
- Frankfurter studied law and used his knowledge to protect people's rights.
- He was part of important decisions on the US Supreme Court.

white children to go to separate schools. But the schools for black children were poor. The court said this wasn't fair. That decision came in 1954.

Frankfurter served on the Supreme Court until 1962. He died in 1965.

Elaine Chao Is First Asian American Woman in Cabinet

Elaine Chao was born in Taipei, Taiwan, in 1953. When she was eight years old, she moved to the United States with her family. At the time, she spoke no English. But she quickly learned.

Chao was a good student. She studied economics and business in college. This education allowed Chao to work for banks. She specialized in lending money to transportation businesses. In 1986, Chao used this experience to get a job in the US Department of Transportation. Three years later, she was named deputy secretary of the department.

After spending some time working outside of the government, Chao returned in historic fashion. President George W. Bush named her to his cabinet in 2001. She was the first Asian American woman to have that honor. The cabinet is a group of people the president chooses to run different parts of the government. Chao's role was Secretary of the Department of Labor. She oversaw how businesses treated their workers.

8

Number of years Elaine Chao served as US Secretary of Labor.

- Chao emigrated from Taiwan with her family when she was eight years old.
- She worked in banking before getting jobs in the US government.
- Chao is the first Asian American woman to serve on a US president's cabinet.

THINK ABOUT IT

Imagine for a moment that you are president of the United States. Who would you pick for your cabinet? Who would be in charge of which tasks?

After heading the Department of Labor, Chao again worked outside the government. She would return, however, in 2017. In that year, President Donald Trump named her to his cabinet. The president asked Chao to lead the Department of Transportation. It was the same department she first worked in as a government official.

Maria Contreras-Sweet Helps American Dreams

Many people who want to start small business have one big problem. They don't have enough money. They are willing to work hard, but they can't get started without a loan.

Maria Contreras-Sweet wanted to help. An immigrant from Mexico, she created a bank in 2006 that helped people start businesses. ProAmérica bank provides loans to small businesses in Southern California. Many bank clients are Latino immigrants pursuing the American dream.

Contreras-Sweet is living an American dream of her own. Born in Guadalajara in 1965, she moved with her family to Los Angeles when she was five years old. She didn't know English when she arrived. But she quickly picked it up and excelled in school.

Contreras-Sweet worked for big businesses after she finished college. She then joined the California governor's cabinet, the first Latina to do so. After leaving that post, Contreras-Sweet created ProAmérica. She also started organizations that helped people manage their money and live healthier lives.

All of this good work got the attention of President Barack

Obama. In 2014, he named Contreras-Sweet to his cabinet. She led the Small Business Administration, helping people get the loans they needed to pursue their dreams of a better life.

THE IMMIGRANT EXPERIENCE

Maria Contreras-Sweet made her American dream come true with hard work and sacrifice. Her family inspired her on this path. Contreras-Sweet remembers her mom working long hours. Her grandmother made clothes for the family. And Contreras-Sweet, along with her siblings, cleaned houses to earn money. This full family effort is common among immigrants to new lands.

3

Number of years Maria Contreras-Sweet served in President Obama's cabinet.

- Contreras-Sweet emigrated from Mexico with her family when she was five.
- She started a bank that helps people start small businesses.
- Contreras-Sweet served as a member of President Barack Obama's cabinet.

Henry Kissinger Improves International Relations

Harvard University. He eventually became a professor at the school. Kissinger taught students about government. He also wrote books on how countries should get along with each other.

Kissinger became well known for his knowledge of foreign policy. During the 1950s and 1960s, US presidents asked his advice on diplomacy. In 1968, President Richard Nixon made Kissinger the National Security Advisor and the Secretary of State. In these roles, Kissinger oversaw US relations with other countries.

During the 1920s and 1930s, Jewish people in Germany were unfairly blamed for the country's problems. This is the world Henry Kissinger grew up in. Then in 1938, when Henry was 15, the Kissinger family moved to the United States to escape persecution.

After serving in the US military, Henry Kissinger attended

Kissinger is remembered as a great diplomat. He helped improve US relationships with several countries. For example, Kissinger met secretly with Chinese leaders to improve relations. He also helped bring the United States and Soviet Union closer together. Kissinger helped end a war between Syria, Egypt, and Israel that

17

Number of books written by Henry Kissinger.

- The Kissinger family emigrated from Germany to escape persecution.
- Kissinger became an expert on how countries should act toward one another.
- He helped improve US relations with several nations around the world.

THINK ABOUT IT

New presidents usually put their own people in important jobs. But President Ford kept Henry Kissinger as Secretary of State, even though Kissinger had worked for Nixon. Why do you think he did? Learn more online.

began in 1973. He helped end the Vietnam War as well.

After Nixon resigned in 1974, Kissinger was National Security Adviser and Secretary of State for President Gerald Ford. He also wrote many books about foreign policy.

Kissinger meeting with Egypt's President Anwar Sadat in 1975.

Tammy Duckworth Serves as Soldier and Politician

2004, Duckworth was sent to fight in the Iraq War. Her helicopter was blown up by enemy fire. Duckworth lost both of her legs. One of her arms was also impaired.

As she healed from her injuries, Duckworth fought to get better medical care for veterans. In 2006, she became director of the Illinois Department of Veterans Affairs. This government office helped soldiers returning home after fighting. In 2009, President Barack Obama named Duckworth Assistant Secretary of US Veteran Affairs. There she helped improve veterans' lives across the country.

Duckworth ran for a seat in the US House of Representatives in 2012. She won the election, representing people in Illinois. Duckworth became the first female soldier disabled in war to serve in the House of Representatives.

Tammy Duckworth was born in 1968 in Thailand. Growing up, she lived in different countries because of her father's work. The family moved to Hawaii when Duckworth was a teenager.

Duckworth attended college at Northern Illinois University. There she joined the military. She became a helicopter pilot. In

123,206
**Number of votes
Tammy Duckworth
received in her election
to the US House.**

- Duckworth lost both of her legs fighting for the United States in Iraq.
- She worked in the government to help former soldiers returning from war.
- Duckworth is the first woman disabled in combat to serve in the US Congress.

THE IRAQ WAR

The United States invaded Iraq in 2003. US leaders believed that the Middle Eastern country was involved in terrorism. Six weeks after the invasion, President George W. Bush said the war was over. But people in some parts of Iraq continued to fight. As of 2018, US troops remain in Iraq. There is less open fighting, but terror attacks there continue.

Arnold Schwarzenegger Goes from Acting to Politics

Arnold Schwarzenegger was born in Thal, Austria, in 1947. He became a bodybuilder. Bodybuilders exercise a lot to build strong muscles.

Schwarzenegger won many bodybuilding awards. He was named Mr. Universe five times and Mr. Olympia six times. A movie was made of him winning a bodybuilding award. It was called *Pumping Iron*. This movie helped him to become a star.

To pursue his acting career, Schwarzenegger moved to the United States in 1968. He made a lot of action movies with stunts and fight scenes. One popular movie was *Terminator*.

Schwarzenegger became involved in American politics in 1990. President George H. W. Bush put him in charge of the President's Council on Physical Fitness and Sports. This program encouraged people to be more active and healthy.

In 2003, Schwarzenegger was elected governor of California. He had never been elected to a government job before. But he was a successful leader. Schwarzennegger was reelected in 2008 and served until 2011. After serving as governor, he went back to making movies and TV shows.

11

Number of major bodybuilding awards won by Arnold Schwarzennegger.

- Schwarzenegger was a bodybuilder who emigrated from Austria to act in movies.
- He starred in action movies like *Terminator*.
- Schwarzenegger served eight years as governor of California.

THINK ABOUT IT

Arnold Schwarzenegger is not the only actor to be governor of California. Ronald Reagan also held the role. Why do you think Californians would elect actors to lead their state?

THE GREAT A

Ilhan Omar Is First Female Somali American Lawmaker

the camp, the Omar family moved to the United States.

Settled in Minneapolis, Minnesota, Omar learned English. She also attended political meetings with her grandfather. She would translate what was being said into Somali. This allowed her grandfather to understand what was happening in the community.

Ilhan Omar was born in Somalia in 1982. She left the Eastern African country with her family when she was eight. People in Somalia were fighting each other in a war. It was not safe to stay there.

Omar's family moved to a refugee camp in Kenya. It was filled with thousands of people who had fled the violence. After living in

4
Number of years Ilhan Omar lived in a refugee camp.

- Omar emigrated from Somalia with her family.
- She became interested in politics after translating speeches for her grandfather.
- Omar is the first woman from Somalia to help make laws in the United States.

Omar was hooked on politics. She started working on campaigns to help people get elected. One was Andrew Johnson. After Johnson won his city election, he hired Omar to help in his office.

But Ilhan Omar wished to win office herself. In 2016, voters elected her to the Minnesota House of Representatives. She became the first female Somali American Muslim lawmaker in the United States.

DADAAB

Families like Omar's are fortunate to make it to the United States. Many others do not get the opportunity to leave Kenyan refugee camps. Nearly a quarter of a million people live in Dadaab, the site of five large camps in Kenya. These people have fled violence and other mistreatment in their home countries.

Dalip Singh Saund Is First Indian American in Congress

Dalip Singh Saund was born in northwestern India in 1899. He immigrated to the United States to attend college in California.

After college, Saund got involved in politics. He wanted people to understand the situation in his native country. Great

Britain ruled India at the time. But Saund thought the country should be independent. He gave speeches in favor of India ruling itself.

Saund also fought injustice in the United States. In the 1940s, Saund helped convince the US Congress to allow Indian immigrants to become citizens. Before that, only European citizens from India could become US citizens. Saund himself became a US citizen in 1949.

During the 1950s, Saund served as a judge on a California court. But his political ambitions were greater. In 1956, Saund became the first Indian American elected to the US Congress. He served for six years in the House of Representatives. His many accomplishments include leading the first meeting between lawmakers from the United States and Mexico.

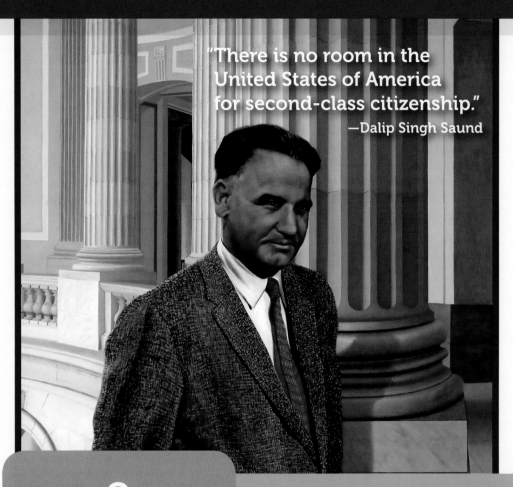

"There is no room in the United States of America for second-class citizenship."
—Dalip Singh Saund

3

Number of two-year terms Dalip Singh Saund served in the US Congress.

- Saund emigrated from India to study at a California college.
- He fought for Indian independence and Indian-American rights.
- Saund became the first Indian American to serve in the US Congress.

GREATER DIVERSITY IN CONGRESS

At the time that Dalip Singh Saund was elected to the US Congress, nearly all members were white men. That has changed dramatically over time. Now Congress is much more diverse. In 2017, 19 percent of members were people of color. This reflects trends in the US population. Additionally, one in five members were women, an all-time high.

After Holocaust, Thomas Lantos Fights for Human Rights

14

Number of terms Thomas Lantos served in the US House of Representatives.

- Lantos spent time in Nazi work camps during World War II.
- After becoming a professor, he began to work in government.
- In Congress, he helped people get fair treatment.

Thomas Lantos was born in 1928 in Budapest, Hungary. Nazis took over Hungary when Lantos was a teen. Because he was Jewish, Lantos was sent to a work camp. People were forced to do hard labor. Many died. But Lantos survived. In fact, he was able to escape. Lantos used fake papers that allowed him to leave the country.

After World War II, Thomas Lantos immigrated to the United States. He went to college in Washington State and then California. Eventually he became a professor.

In the 1970s, Lantos began working in government as an aide to politicians. After supporting elected officials, Lantos decided to run for public office himself. In 1980, he was elected to represent California citizens in the US House of Representatives.

Rep. Tom Lantos touches foreheads with the Dalai Lama.

Human rights were important to Lantos. He had suffered abuses in the Nazi work camp. He used his position to help make sure governments around the world treated their people fairly.

Lantos is the first and only Holocaust survivor to have served in the US Congress.

In 2018, this statue of Lantos was inaugurated in Budapest, Hungary.

THE HOLOCAUST

The Holocaust took place in the late 1930s and early 1940s in Europe. The Nazis took over Germany and other countries. Nazis hated Jewish people. They put them in camps along with other people they didn't like. The Nazis forced people in the camps to work. They also killed prisoners, including six million Jews.

More Immigrants in History

ALBERT GALLATIN

Albert Gallatin.

Albert Gallatin

Alexander Hamilton was not the only US Secretary of the Treasury born outside the country. Albert Gallatin was born in Geneva, Switzerland. He became the fourth treasury secretary. He held the job from 1801 to 1814. That is longer than any other person.

Charles August Lindbergh

The father of famous airplane pilot Charles A. Lindbergh Jr. was a member of the US House of Representatives. Charles August Lindbergh Sr. was born in Stockholm, Sweden, in 1859. He moved to Minnesota with his parents the next year. Lindbergh's son flew the first solo nonstop flight across the Atlantic Ocean in 1927.

Zbigniew
Brzezinski advising
President Jimmy
Carter in 1977.

Zbigniew Brzezinski

Born in Poland, Zbigniew Brzezinski was an expert on international relations. He gave advice to presidents John F. Kennedy and Lyndon B. Johnson about how the United States should treat other countries. He was President Jimmy Carter's National Security Adviser from 1977 to 1981.

Jerry Springer

Jerry Springer was born in London, England. He moved to New York City with his family when he was five. When Jerry grew up, he was elected mayor of Cincinnati, Ohio. He ran the city from 1977 to 1978. After being mayor, Springer became a TV star.

Editor's note:
America is a nation of immigrants. This series celebrates important contributions immigrants have made to politics. In choosing the people to feature in this book, the author and 12-Story Library editors considered diversity of all kinds and the significance and stature of the work.

Glossary

cabinet
A group of powerful people who help the leader of a government make decisions.

communism
A system of governing in which all property is publicly owned.

diplomat
A person who represents a country in talks with other nations, or diplomacy.

foreign policy
The plans a government makes to deal with other countries.

government
The group of people who officially run a country.

immigrant
A person who leaves one country to live in another.

integrate
To bring together. To end a system or policy that keeps people apart because of race or color.

international relations
The study of how nations get along with one another.

persecution
Cruel or unfair treatment of a person or group because of race, religion, or political beliefs.

ratify
To make an agreement or treaty official, usually by voting for it or signing it.

refugee camp
A place people live after fleeing violence or persecution in their homeland.

representative
A person chosen by voters to make choices for them in government.

veteran
Someone who has completed military service.

For More Information

Books

Brown, D. *Aaron and Alexander: The Most Famous Duel in American History.* New York: Roaring Book Press, 2015.

Lowery, Z. Democracy. *Political and Economic Systems.* New York: Rosen Education Service, 2014.

Weis, R. *The US Congress for Kids: Over 200 Years of Lawmaking, Deal-Breaking, and Compromising.* Chicago: Chicago Review Press, 2014.

Visit 12StoryLibrary.com

Scan the code or use your school's login at **12StoryLibrary.com** for recent updates about this topic and a full digital version of this book. Enjoy free access to:

- Digital ebook
- Breaking news updates
- Live content feeds
- Videos, interactive maps, and graphics
- Additional web resources

Note to educators: Visit 12StoryLibrary.com/register to sign up for free premium website access. Enjoy live content plus a full digital version of every 12-Story Library book you own for every student at your school.

Index

About the Author

Diane Marczely Gimpel is an English and social studies teacher. Also the author of books, she is a former newspaper reporter. Diane lives near Philadelphia, Pennsylvania, with her husband and their two sons.

READ MORE FROM 12-STORY LIBRARY

Every 12-Story Library Book is available in many fomats. For more information, visit 12StoryLibrary.com